ST. BONIFACE SCHOOL
Waumandee, Wisconsin

Better Homes and Gardens®
IT'S A SPECIAL DAY

Hi! My name is Max. I have some great projects to show you—and they're all about special days! We're going to have lots of fun making them together.

© Copyright 1988 by Meredith Corporation, Des Moines, Iowa.
All Rights Reserved. Printed in the United States of America.
First Edition. Third Printing, 1989.
ISBN: 0-696-01899-3 (hard cover)
ISBN: 0-696-01812-8 (trade paperback)
MAX THE DRAGON™ and other characters in this book are trademarks and copyrighted characters of Meredith Corporation, and their use by others is strictly prohibited.

ST. BONIFACE SCHOOL
Waumandee, Wisconsin

Inside You'll Find...

Let's Have a Party! 4
You'll have a good time playing a find-the-object game at Max's birthday party.

Birthday Bundles 6
For party favors, wrap cardboard tubes like presents and fill them with delicious surprises.

Party Hats 8
Paper, hat decorations, and imagination are all you need to make a great party hat.

Soda-Fountain Cakes 10
Bake cupcakes in ice-cream cones. Then frost and decorate them for a perfect party treat.

Let's Go Fishing! 12
Max is on a fishing trip and needs your help to find the fish.

Fishin' for Fun 14
You can have a favorite fishing spot right at home by making these fish and a fishing pole.

Nibblin' Fish 16
This easy snack is stocked with fish crackers, pretzels, nuts, and cereal.

Let's Have a Picnic!............ 18
Go on a picnic with Max and try to guess the answers to his silly riddles.

Apple Smiles...................... 20
Turn apples, peanut butter, and marshmallows into a great picnic snack.

Picnic Peekaboo Box......... 22
Mother Nature supplies the materials and you supply the shoe box for this clever project.

Let's Clown Around!.......... 24
Max is dressed like a clown and wants you to find the differences between the two pictures.

Clown-Around Masks......... 26
Turn a paper plate into a funny clown face and pretend you're in the circus.

Make Funny Faces............. 28
Make a face that changes quickly when you move its mouth back and forth.

Parents' Pages.................... 30
A special section with more activities, suggestions for books to read aloud, and helpful hints for making projects successful.

A birthday bash and a find-the-object game.

Let's Have a Party!

Hip hip hooray! Max is having a surprise birthday party. In the picture are some surprises for you. Can you find all the things in the picture that begin with the letter B?

More Birthday Fun

Did you know that when things aren't the same they are different? Look at the pictures below and find the differences.

Which present is the biggest?
Which present is the smallest?

Which candle is the tallest?
Which candle is the shortest?

Which glass is full?
Which glass is empty?

Festive tubes filled with birthday goodies.

Birthday Bundles

Invite your friends over to your house for a birthday party and let each one make a Birthday Bundle. Fill the bundles with candy, popcorn, or small toys.

What you'll need...
- 4½-inch cardboard tubes
- Tissue paper, cut into 10x13-inch pieces
- Tape
- Crinkle ribbon or yarn, cut into 12-inch pieces
- Candy, popcorn, or small toys
- Scissors

1 Place one cardboard tube near the short edge of one piece of tissue paper. Roll paper up around the tube (see photo).

2 Tape the tissue paper to keep it rolled around the tube. Tie one end of the tissue paper with ribbon (see photo).

3 Fill the open end of the cardboard tube with candy (see photo). Tie the open end of the tissue paper with ribbon.
   With adult help, curl the ribbon with scissors, or tie the yarn in a bow.

Any-Day Bundles

Birthdays aren't the only days you can enjoy these party favors. Bundle up some goodies for May Day, the Fourth of July, Halloween, or any day that's special.

7

Hats for every celebration.

Party Hats

What's a party without party hats? Decorate your hat with crayons, glitter, or balloons to make it special.

What you'll need...
- Scissors
- Construction paper, cut into a 9-inch circle
- Hat Decorations
- Staples or tape
- Pencil
- Two 24-inch pieces of yarn

Hat Decorations
Make your hat look just the way you like. See the hats below for ideas, or make up your own. Paint, rickrack, and adhesive stickers all make great hat decorations.

1 Cut a wedge from the circle of paper. The wedge should be about ¼ of the circle.

2 Decorate the paper any way you like. (See tip at left for Hat Decorations.)

3 Join the cut edges of the paper to make a cone. Overlap the ends about 1 inch. Staple the ends together.

4 With adult help, use a pencil to poke 1 hole on each side of the paper. Insert yarn. Knot the end of each piece of yarn to secure it in hole.

Clever cupcakes baked in ice-cream cones.

Soda-Fountain Cakes

Looks like ice cream—tastes like cake.

What you'll need...
- Cake mix batter for a 1-layer-size cake
- 1-cup glass measure
- 12 flat-bottom cones
- Muffin pan or large baking pan
- Plastic or table knife
- 2 cups canned frosting
- Cupcake Toppers (see tip on page 11)

1 With adult help, pour some of the batter into the glass measure. Pour batter into cones (see photo). Fill each cone so the batter is about 1 inch from the top. Refill glass measure with batter and fill remaining cones. Place ice cream cones in a muffin pan.

2 With adult help, bake filled cones in a 350° oven for 30 minutes. Cool on a wire rack.
  Using a knife, frost tops of cakes with frosting (see photo).

3 Decorate each frosted cone with Cupcake Toppers.

Cupcake Toppers

Top your Soda Fountain Cake with assorted candy, miniature semisweet chocolate pieces, or chopped nuts. To make your cupcake look like a soda, snip two 3-inch pieces from a straw and stick them into the frosting.

A find-the-fish picture game.

Let's Go Fishing!

One fine sunny day, Max grabbed his fishing pole and went fishing. But when he got to his favorite fishing spot, he couldn't catch any fish. Can you help Max find the 10 fish?

ST. BONIFACE SCHOOL

Catch a paper-plate fish right in your living room.

Fishin' for Fun

You can go fishing at your house anytime you like. Just grab a paper plate, yarn, foil, and a stick. That's all you need for a whole day of fishing fun. But hurry up—the fish are biting!

What you'll need...
- Paper-Plate Fish (see page 31)
- Tissue paper, torn into small pieces, or crayons
- White crafts glue or paste
- One 6x12-inch piece of foil
- One 12-inch piece of yarn or string
- Stick, about 20 inches long

1 Lay your Paper-Plate Fish flat. Glue pieces of tissue paper to the plate to look like fish scales (see photo). Or color the plate any color you like.

2 To make the fishing hook, crumple and shape the foil to look like a hook.

3 Tie one end of the yarn to the foil hook. Tie the other end of the yarn to the stick (see photo).
   Now you're ready to fish! Stand your fish up on the floor. Then hold the fishing pole and try to get the foil hook through the fish's eye.

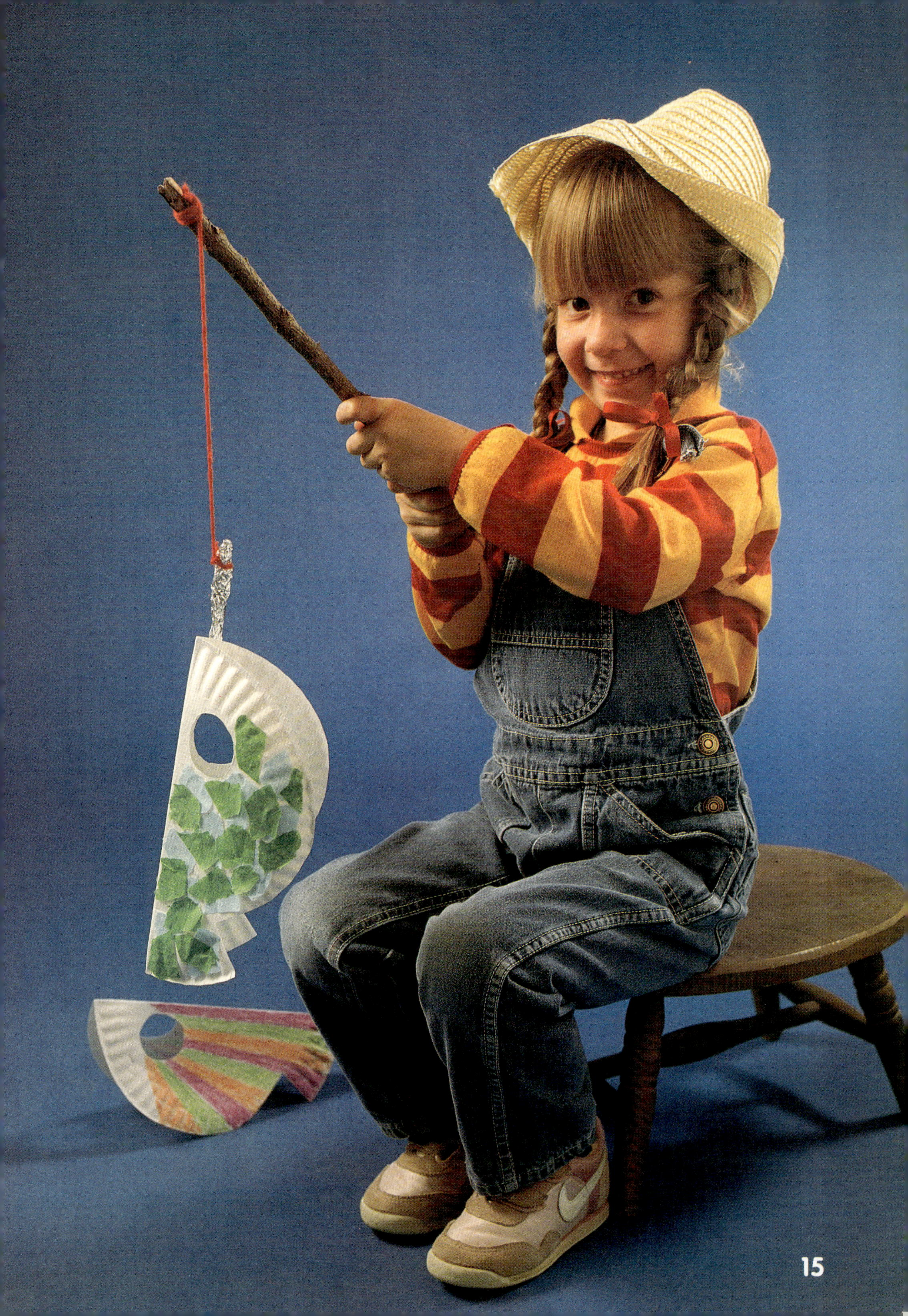

A toss-together snack mix.

Nibblin' Fish

Are you hungry and fishing for a nibble? Then use pretzel sticks to catch the fish-shaped crackers. The nuts are stones for the fish to hide behind, and the cereal rounds are air bubbles.

What you'll need...
- 1 medium paper sack or large plastic bag
- 2½ cups round toasted oat cereal
- 1½ cups pretzel sticks
- 1 cup small fish-shaped crackers
- 1 cup mixed nuts or peanuts

In a paper sack combine cereal, pretzel sticks, crackers, and nuts. Close the end of the bag. Shake well.

What's the best way to talk to a fish?

Drop him a line!

Tail

Fin

Scales

Gill

Did you know...

- A fish uses its gills and mouth to breathe in the water.
- A fish uses its tail to swim. It moves its tail from side to side. This helps push the fish forward. Do you like to swim? A fish does! Fish are the best swimmers in the world.
- Fins help a fish steer itself as it swims. Some fish, like flatfish and sea horses, use their side fins to move. Other fish can even wiggle like snakes or "walk" on their fins.
- The skin of fish is different from your skin. Most fish are covered with scales. These scales protect their soft bodies. A few fish actually are covered with hard bony scales that feel like fingernails.

Riddles and a poem to start a picnic off right.

Let's Have a Picnic!

Max likes to go on picnics and eat peanut butter sandwiches. But guess what? Ants like peanut butter, too!

Here are some riddles that Max likes to tell when he's on a picnic:

What's the best way to catch a squirrel?

Climb up a tree and act like a nut.

Why do birds fly south in the winter?

Because it's too far to walk.

What's white on the outside, brown and green on the inside, and hops?

A peanut butter and frog sandwich.

18

Peanut Butter

Max loves peanuts,
And Max loves butter.
But what he loves the most
Is chunky peanut butter.

He spreads it on his toast,
And he spreads it on his nose.
He even likes to spread it
Between his chubby toes!

He eats it in the morning,
And he eats it in the dark.
He even likes to eat it
At a picnic in the park.

But one day on his picnic,
(An anthill wasn't far!)
While Max munched peanut butter,
Ants ran off with his jar!

A lip-smacking picnic treat.

Apple Smiles

This funny-looking snack has apple-slice lips, peanut butter gums, and marshmallow teeth. It makes a great-tasting smile!

What you'll need...
- Table knife
- Red apple, cored and sliced
- Peanut butter
- Tiny marshmallows

1 Using a table knife, spread one side of each apple slice with peanut butter. Be sure to use plenty of peanut butter so the marshmallows will stick.

2 Place 3 or 4 tiny marshmallows on top of the peanut butter on 1 apple slice (see photo). Top with another apple slice, peanut butter side down. Squeeze gently. Eat right away.

Pack a Picnic

Apple Smiles are great for a picnic, but save room for more goodies. Other take-along picnic foods are popcorn, nuts, vegetables, cheese, and fruit juice. Pack them in a picnic basket with plenty of napkins and paper plates.

Max brought along a basket of juicy apples on his picnic. How many apples are there?

Sticks and stones become a picnic scene.

Picnic Peekaboo Box

The next time you're on a picnic, pick up sticks, gather acorns, look for leaves, poke around for pebbles, and fetch a flower. Then use these treasures in your own Picnic Peekaboo Box.

What you'll need...
- Crayons
- Empty shoe box
- White crafts glue, paste, or modeling clay
- Picnic treasures
- Cotton balls
- Scissors
- White tissue paper
- Tape

1 Color the inside of the box. Glue your picnic treasures onto the bottom of the box (see photo). For fluffy clouds, glue cotton balls around the inside top edge of the box.

2 With adult help, cut a rectangular opening out of one end of the box. This will be the peek hole.
Cut a piece of tissue paper large enough to cover the top of the box. Fold edges of paper around box. Tape paper to the sides of the box (see photo).

3 Now look inside the box through the peek hole. What do you see?

22

23

Discover what's different in these two pictures.

Let's Clown Around!

Max is dressed up like a silly clown. Look closely at the two pictures. They are not exactly alike. Can you find the 12 things that are different?

24

ST. BONIFACE SCHOOL
Waumandee, Wisconsin

Playful masks made from paper plates.

Clown-Around Masks

Everyone loves watching a silly clown. You can pretend you're a clown in the circus by making a clown mask. What will your mask look like?

What you'll need...
- Scissors
- Paper plate
- Crayons
- White crafts glue
- Face Decorations (see tip on page 27)
- Tape
- Crafts stick or straw

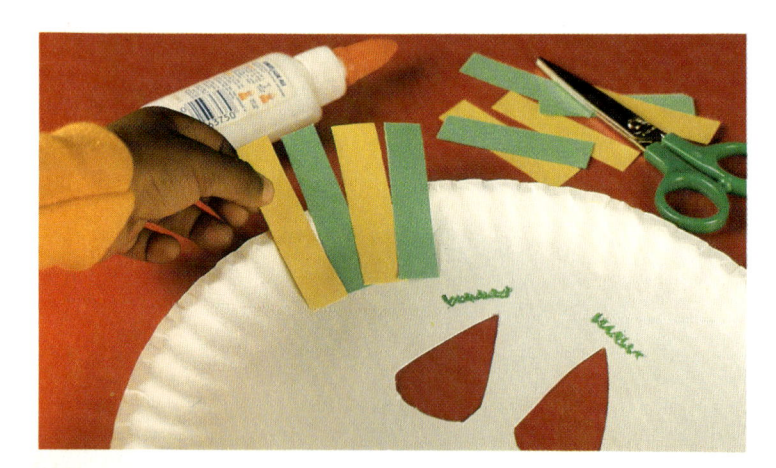

1 If you like, cut two holes out of the plate for eyes. Draw a nose and mouth on the plate. Color or glue face decorations on the plate (see photo).

2 For the handle, turn the paper plate over. Tape a crafts stick to the back of the plate (see photo).

3 Max is huffing and puffing to blow up a balloon. He thinks it will make a great nose for one of his Clown-Around Masks. Can you find the mask on the next page that has a balloon nose?

26

Face Decorations

Crayons work great for putting on a colorful clown face. Markers, colored pencils, and even paint are good choices for making your mask. Or, use construction paper, yarn, balloons, or cotton balls to decorate the face.

27

Who can draw the funniest face with paper and crayons?

Make Funny Faces

Make a face that looks happy, sad, or surprised just by changing its mouth. All you need for your new friend's face are construction paper, scissors, and crayons.

What you'll need...
- Crayons or markers
- One sheet of construction paper
- Scissors
- One 3½x12-inch strip of construction paper

1 Draw two eyes and a nose on the sheet of construction paper (see photo). Remember to leave room at the bottom of the paper for the mouth.

2 Cut two vertical slits (up-and-down cuts) into the construction paper just below the nose. Make the slits about 3 inches apart and about 4 inches long. Slide the strip of construction paper into the slits (see photo).

3 Draw a mouth on the strip of construction paper. Slide the strip until the first mouth is hidden. Draw another mouth (see photo). Slide the strip again and draw a third mouth.

Now move the strip of paper back and forth to make three funny faces.

Here are more funny-face ideas.

Parents' Pages

We've filled this special section with more activities, recipes, reading recommendations, hints we learned from our kid-testers, and many other helpful tips.

Let's Have a Party!

See pages 4 and 5

Children love parties—especially birthday parties. For the next one at your house, serve the thirsty gang one of these festive sippers. They were a big hit with our kid-testers.

Lickety-Split Lemonade:
Combine one 12-ounce can *frozen lemonade concentrate*, 3 cups *water*, and ¼ cup *honey*. Stir till well combined. If desired, pour over ice in sugar-rimmed glasses. Makes about 6 (6-ounce) servings.

Banana-Berry Slush:
In a blender container combine one 6-ounce can frozen *limeade or lemonade concentrate*, one thawed 10-ounce package *frozen strawberries*, and 1 medium *banana*, cut up. Cover and blend till smooth. With blender running, add ice cubes, one at a time, through opening in lid till blender is full. Makes about 6 (6-ounce) servings.

Quick Minty Cocoa:
In a large saucepan heat 9 cups *water* till warm. Stir in 2¾ cups *instant cocoa mix* and ⅓ cup *buttermints*, crushed. Stir till blended. Cool slightly. Top with *pressurized dessert topping* and *miniature semisweet chocolate pieces*. Makes 12 (6-ounce) servings.

Birthday Bundles

See pages 6 and 7

Our kid-testers thought these party favors were the greatest. Some of the younger children preferred using coding labels instead of tape to fasten the tissue paper to the cardboard tube. When the kids finished making their bundles, they wrote their names on them.

If cardboard tubes aren't available, let your children make these bundles with foil. Simply tear off a 10x12-inch piece of foil. Starting at one of the short sides, roll up the foil to make a cylinder about 2 inches in diameter. Continue as directed on page 6.

Party Hats

See pages 8 and 9

A quick way to make a 9-inch circle for this project is to trace around a paper plate on the construction paper. Or, simply use the paper plate for the hat.

Soda-Fountain Cakes

See pages 10 and 11

If you're looking for a big-hit birthday treat for your next party, look no further. Our kid-testers devoured these cakes in minutes. And the ice-cream cones are easy for children to hold while they eat the frosting and cake.

Before you begin making these, here are a few tips:

- Look for holes in the ice-cream cones. Even very small holes will allow the batter to leak out during baking.
- Don't overfill the cones with batter. If you fill them too full, the batter may run over the sides of the cones during baking. If this happens, simply scrape off any excess, cool, and frost.
- You can make these treats the day ahead. Just store the baked and cooled cones, uncovered, at room temperature. Do not put them in a tightly covered container or they will become soft and sticky. Frost and decorate the cones up to a few hours before serving.

Let's Go Fishing!

See pages 12 and 13

Fish are as much fun to watch as they are to catch. A fishbowl is an easy and inexpensive way to interest your children in fish as pets. Once your children are familiar with caring for a fish in a fishbowl, they can graduate to an aquarium. And setting up a fish aquarium is relatively simple.

A pet store is a good source of aquarium information. Read pamphlets and books at the pet store (or go to the library) to learn as much as you can about aquariums. Talk to your children about the responsibilities of owning fish and taking care of them and their environment.

The store clerk is a good person to consult about your aquarium needs. The clerk can help you choose all the components needed to start an aquarium.

When you're ready to buy your fish, again ask the clerk for advice. You'll want to know how many fish to start with and which fish live well together in the same tank.

Fishin' for Fun

See pages 14 and 15

This project made a big splash with our kid-testers. The children had trouble cutting out the eyes and tail for the fish, so we suggest that you do this step. Here's how you can make the Paper-Plate Fish:
- Fold one paper plate in half.
- With a sharp scissors, poke a hole in the folded plate. Cut a hole to make two eyes.
- Then, at the opposite end, cut out a notch to resemble a fish tail.

Nibblin' Fish

See pages 16 and 17

This nibble mix is perfect for kids to make. You can customize the cereal, crackers, and nuts for your children's tastes.
- Reading suggestions:
Swimmy
   by Leo Lionni
A Fish Out of Water
   by Helen Palmer
The Gillygoofang
   by George Mendoza

Let's Have a Picnic!

See pages 18 and 19

A picnic featuring peanut butter is fun for children and easy for adults. Go beyond the basic peanut butter sandwich with these sandwich combinations.
- Make a "monkey sandwich" by combining peanut butter and chopped banana.
- Entice children with a "bunny bite" by mixing together peanut butter and shredded carrot or chopped celery.
- Make a "tropical treat" with peanut butter, crushed pineapple, and coconut.
- Make an "apple lover's sandwich" with peanut butter and shredded apple and cheese.
- Try a "nutty apple sandwich" with peanut butter, raisins, applesauce, and nutmeg.

Apple Smiles

See pages 20 and 21

This simple recipe for Apple Smiles is great to take along for a picnic or a quick-to-fix snack. If you plan to make these ahead, lightly brush each apple slice with lemon juice to prevent the apples from turning brown.

Picnic Peekaboo Box

See pages 22 and 23

Your children don't need to go on a picnic to make this project. There are lots of interesting "treasures" for them to find at home. Have them look in their own backyard or in the house. Encourage them to gather items that have different shapes and textures, such as feathers, coins, weeds, dry cereal, or miniature toys.

Kid Clowns

Every clown has his or her own special face that is not copied by other clowns. Let your children create their own clown faces with makeup.

Ask your children to describe how they want to look as clowns. Then start by applying zinc oxide salve to their faces to make a white base. Zinc oxide salve is available at a pharmacy or theatrical shop.

Rub the salve on smoothly and evenly, blending it into their skin. Next decide where you will apply color. Using the makeup, begin face painting.

If something doesn't look right, gently rub the makeup off with baby oil and try to draw something else.

Here are some easy face-painting ideas:
- With red lipstick, apply a large red smiling mouth and then outline it with a black eyeliner pencil.
- Use an eyeliner pencil or eye shadow pencil to draw dark, wavy eyebrows.
- With bright pink rouge or lipstick, make a circle on each cheek.
- Draw a diamond or square around each eye with a colorful eye shadow pencil or lipstick.

Here are a few more face-painting tips: Don't use wax crayons, felt-tip markers, or any type of paint for makeup. These materials may irritate skin. If necessary, tie long hair back in a ponytail before you begin applying the makeup.

Let's Clown Around!

See pages 24 and 25

This circus activity is not only fun, but it helps your children visually discriminate between two drawings. Take this exercise a step further and ask them to match familiar objects at home.
- Enlist your children's help on laundry and cleaning days by having them match pairs of socks and shoes.
- Collect some spoons (serving, wooden, and measuring spoons) that are similar but not exactly alike. Can your children tell the difference?
- Look in a catalog and let your children point to objects that are the same and to the ones that are different.

Clown-Around Masks

See pages 26 and 27

Paper plates are great for making funny clown faces because they're readily available, inexpensive, and easy for children to color. Suggest that your children act out a play using their masks. Or, let them pretend they're in a circus. What would they do to make the audience laugh?

Make Funny Faces

See pages 28 and 29

Encourage your children to express their feelings. Along with making Funny Faces, ask your children what *their* faces look like when they're happy, sad, and surprised. Ask them why they feel this way.

BETTER HOMES AND GARDENS® BOOKS
Editor: Gerald M. Knox
Art Director: Ernest Shelton
Managing Editor: David Kirchner
Department Head, Food and Family Life: Sharyl Heiken

IT'S A SPECIAL DAY
Editors: Sandra Granseth and Linda Foley Woodrum
Editorial Project Manager: Rosanne Weber Mattson
Graphic Designers: Harjis Priekulis and Linda Ford Vermie
Contributing Illustrator: Buck Jones
Contributing Photographer: Scott Little

Have BETTER HOMES AND GARDENS® magazine delivered to your door. For information, write to:
ROBERT AUSTIN
P.O. BOX 4536
DES MOINES, IA 50336